WEB PAGE CREATION AND DESIGN

Linda Ericksen
Lane Community College

Prentice
Hall

Upper Saddle River New Jersey 07458

▶

The programs and applications presented in this book have been
included for their instructional value. They have been tested with
care but are not guaranteed for any particular purpose. The publisher
does not offer any warranties or representations, nor does it accept
any liabilities with respect to the programs or applications.

Prentice
Hall

7 8 9 10
ISBN 0-13-090125-3

CONTENTS

PREFACE

This book was written to accompany and enhance computer concepts texts by providing practical hands-on coverage of Web page design and creation. Students can use this guide to help them complete lab assignments in which they develop a Web site. This book provides guidelines for creating and publishing successful Web documents using HTML and JavaScript. The book is intended for students who are new to creating Web documents from scratch using HTML. However, because of the inclusion of the introduction to JavaScript, students who are more advanced will also find it useful.

Features of the book include:

- Step-by-step instructions with HTML and JavaScript code listings
- Instructions on planning a Web document, evaluating the impact of a document, and publishing a document
- Screen captures of key instructions
- A table of alphabetized HTML tags and attributes used in the book so that students will be more likely to try various options when creating their documents
- A Try This! section at the end of every chapter with suggestions for student projects

I have used this book successfully in my CIS 120 Concepts of Information Processing course at the University of Oregon, and I hope you find it useful as well.

Linda Ericksen

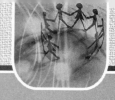

OVERVIEW OF WEB PUBLISHING

BROWSING THE WORLD WIDE WEB

The World Wide Web, also known as the Web or WWW, is the Internet service that has revolutionized communications in the '90s. Prior to the early 1990s university staff, government employees, and military personnel who were doing research or had computer expertise were the only people who used the Internet extensively. Now millions of users are surfing or browsing the Web and even publishing their own Web pages.

In 1989, Tim Berners-Lee at CERN, the European Laboratory for Particle Physics in Geneva, Switzerland, developed a new set of standards for exchanging information on the Internet. The World Wide Web provided a way to link documents on any computer on any network. The release in 1992 of the World Wide Web, based on public specifications, has allowed everyone to develop Web pages.

The World Wide Web is a web of documents on servers-computers all over the world. They are linked by hypertext. That is, the user clicks on a "hot" spot in the document, and he is transferred to the linked document. Hypertext, which is the hot text, contains the invisible address of the computer where the linked document resides and generally appears underlined and in a different color from the surrounding text.

Software, known as a browser, is needed to find and process the hypertext links. The early browsers were text based. In 1993, the National Center for Computing Applications (NCSA) released Mosaic, developed by Marc Andreessen and others at the University of Illinois at Champaign-Urbana. Mosaic was the first graphical Web browser, allowing users to transfer graphics and text. Since the release of the first graphical browser, the Web has become the communications phenomenon of the late 20th century with businesses and individuals wanting a presence on the Web.

This linking of any document to any other document allows for nonlinear, non-sequential communications. That is, rather than having to progress through information one page after another as you do with a book, the user browses through the information by clicking on hypertext or hypermedia (which includes video and audio clips) in the document. In this way, the user is able to read the information in any order rather than in a pre-defined order.

The information on the Web resides on host computers known as Web servers. The computer on your desk, from which you access information on the World Wide Web, is known as the client.

The client computer, which is running a browser, requests the linked document. The protocol or standard that enables the transfer of the request and the subsequent transfer of the linked document is HTTP, Hypertext Transfer Protocol.

Linking to any of millions of Web documents that are on thousands of different servers in thousands of locations requires an addressing scheme. Each network has a unique address and each computer on the network has an address based on the network to which it's connected. The address, based on the Internet Protocol (IP), appears as a long string of numbers separated by periods, for example 198.168.37.186. Because the long numeric IPs are so hard for users to deal with, most networks also have domain names, which are converted into the numeric IP by software. The domain names are words separated by periods, for example, efn.org. In this example, org is the top-level domain name (or suffix) and efn is the second-level domain name. The suffix of the domain name specifies the type of organization to which the computer belongs. Table 1.1 lists the common suffixes.

Table 1.1 COMMON SUFFIXES

SUFFIX	TYPE OF ORGANIZATION
edu	Educational institution
com	Commercial organization
gov	Government
mil	Military
org	Nonprofit organization
net	Networks

Frequently, the domain name also has a suffix that identifies the country in which the server is located. For example, au tells you that the document is located on a server in Australia, as in the address: http://www.freenet.org.au/index.html.

When a user requests a document by clicking a link, a Domain Name Server (DNS) matches the domain name with the IP numeric address. Once the address of the Web server is known, the IP protocol checks with the router—a computer on the Internet that finds routes for the packets of information to travel.

For this addressing scheme to work, each Web site must have a unique domain name, and somebody must keep track of all the domain names. The InterNIC Registration Service approves unique names and keeps track of domain names.

The address of a document, known as its URL-Uniform Resource Locator, appears as the following address for the White House:

http://www.whitehouse.gov/WH/Welcome.html

In this example, http: names the protocol used and tells the browser how to deal with the document. The protocol is usually separated from the second part, the domain name, with two forward slashes (/). The domain name often begins with the three characters www to signify that the document is on a Web server. The last part of the URL (preceded by a single forward slash) is the path or folder on the server where the file is located, and subfolders may be part of this path. The file name of the desired file is the last part of the URL. If no file name is specified, the URL refers to the default file in that folder.

The example just cited tells the browser to use the Hypertext Transfer Protocol (http) to transfer the document that is located on the host computer www.whitehouse.gov in the folder WH with the file name Welcome, and the document is a hypertext document (.html). The three-letter extension htm is also used.

Because the document name in a URL is case sensitive, you must type carefully. Also be sure to include the punctuation exactly, and never include spaces. If you type the example address

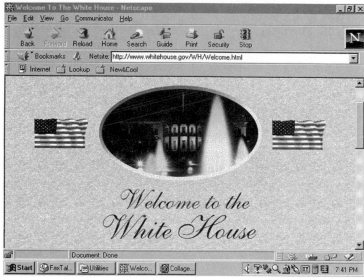

Figure 1.1   Welcome to the White House

correctly into your browser location text box, you will be connected to the White House (see figure 1.1).

The document that appears on the client's screen is called the home page, which is simply the top or first page in a Web document.

USING BROWSER SOFTWARE

Your computer must have browser software to access documents on the Web. The Web server transfers the information to the browser, and then the connection is broken. Each request by the client computer using a browser requires a new, separate connection to the Web server. This is different from maintaining a continuous connection as dumb terminals, terminals with no computing ability, maintain to host computers. Another feature that is unique to browsers is when your browser loads a Web page, it keeps a copy for a limited period of time in a memory location called a cache. When you decide to return to that page, the document may be loaded very fast if it is loaded from the cache not the distant Web server.

Each browser displays Web documents in a unique way. That is, someone using Internet Explorer will see a Web page displayed differently than someone using Netscape Communicator. However, both displays will be similar.

The first generation of text browsers is rapidly being replaced by a second generation of graphical browsers. All these newer browsers allow you to click on links and then to move back to the previous displayed page or move back to your opening page. Browsers allow you to open files by typing in the correct URL, and they also allow you to print the Web document. Browsers allow you to set bookmarks to mark any page that you want to return to at a later time. Bookmarks are maintained by the browser even after you turn off your computer.

While you are on-line with the browser loaded, a history list of the last documents that you displayed is maintained. You can quickly move to a document directly, rather than moving back one Web page at a time by selecting a site from the history list. Loading pages with graphics can be slow, and you might want to speed up the process by not taking the time to load graphics. You do not have to use a different browser; you simply set your graphical browser to load pages as text only.

Many pages will contain forms for the user to receive more information or to simply place your name on a mailing list. Your browser displays the form and takes the data that you type into the form and sends the user an e-mail that contains the contents of the form.

The two most popular browsers today are Netscape Communicator and Microsoft Internet Explorer.

Figure 1.2 shows Netscape's home page, the NetCenter, using the Netscape Communicator 4 browser to display it.

Figure 1.3 shows Microsoft's home page, using the Internet Explorer 4 browser to display it.

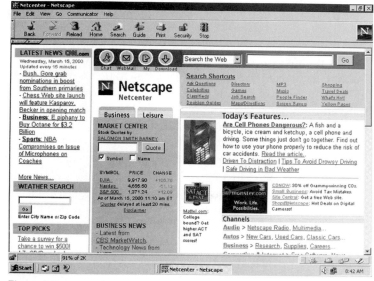

Figure 1.2   www.netscape.com

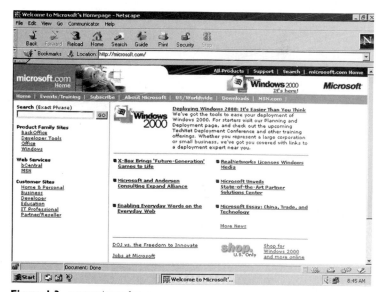

Figure 1.3   www.microsoft.com

UNDERSTANDING HTML

Web pages are made up of text and graphics you want to display, along with links to other documents. You use HTML (Hypertext Markup Language) to provide information to browsers as to how to display pages and create links. HTML is the Web's universal programming language; it's not specific to any platform, computer brand, or operating system. It's a simple programming language that places codes or tags in a Web document, providing information to browsers about the structure of the document.

HTML, developed in 1989, is actually a simplified version of the programming language SGML, short for Standard Generalized Markup Language, which was developed to share documents on different types of computers. HTML contains one added feature: the use of hypertext to link documents.

The first version of HTML contained only about 30 commands (tags), which the user embedded in a document. The next versions expanded the capability of the language to include interactive, dynamic Web sites.

HTML documents are actually ASCII (text) files with HTML tags embedded. HTML tags tell browsers how to display the document; however, each browser expresses the commands in its own way. For example, if you define a line of text on your Web page as a heading, each browser that displays the document knows to display the line of text as a heading. However, each browser might embellish the text in the heading differently, so your Web document will look different when displayed in different browsers.

For any Web page that you display in your browser, you display the HTML by having the browser display the source code. Figure 1.4 displays a Web document, and Figure 1.5 displays the source code.

To view the source code in Netscape, choose View|Page Source. To view the source code using Internet Explorer, choose View|Source.

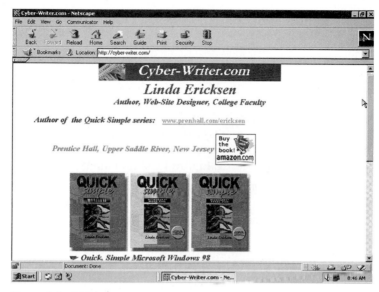

Figure 1.4   A Web document

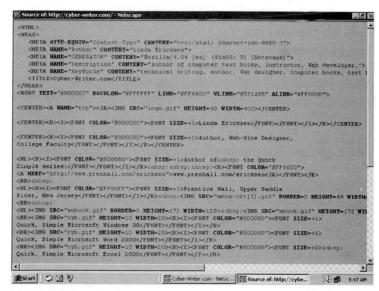

Figure 1.5   Source code

CREATING WEB PAGES WITH AN EDITOR

There are numerous ways to create documents for the World Wide Web. You can use your word processor, such as Word for Office 97 to create a document as you ordinarily would and then choose File|Save as HTML. This option will place all of the HTML tags into your document for you. A second approach that you can use to create Web documents with Word for Office 97 is to create the Web page using a Microsoft Wizard. Choose File|New|Web Pages|Web Page Wizard.wiz. Figure 1.6 shows the Wizard.

If you are using Netscape Communicator, you can use Netscape Composer to create your pages. From Navigator, choose Communicator|Page Composer. The Netscape Composer displays, as shown in Figure 1.7.

Using Netscape Communicator, you can create a Web document from scratch, or you can use one of the built-in templates or even get the Page Wizard to help you create your page.

Figure 1.6   Word wizard

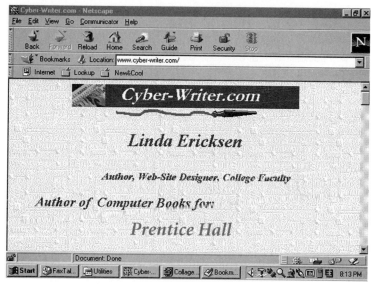

Figure 1.7   Netscape Composer

Other Web editors that are popular include FrontPage, Hot-Dog Professional, HotMetal Pro, or WebEdit Professional.

CREATING WEB PAGES WITH HTML

If you want to code your pages from scratch, you can use Windows Notepad. Simply click the Start menu and choose Programs|Accessories|Notepad. Figure 1.8 shows a file in Notepad with the Save As dialog box displayed.

When you save an HTML document in Notepad, include the extension .html or .htm and change the Save as Type option to All Files (*.*).

No matter what approach you take to creating your Web documents, you will need to be familiar with HTML. As pages become more complex and interactive, you will want to be able to solve problems, tweak appearances, and learn to include new fea-

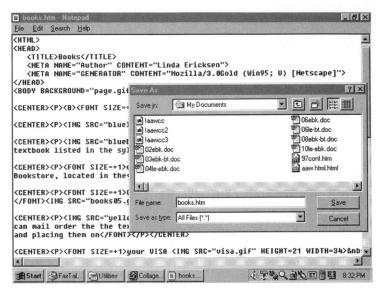

Figure 1.8   Notepad

tures on your pages. In order to do so, you will need to do more than have a Wizard crank out a Web document for you. So learning to use HTML is not just information for a course, but a tool that will come in handy in your personal and work world.

PLANNING A WEB PAGE

Because anyone can publish on the Web, you'll see all kinds of poorly designed, hard-to-read pages. So before you begin creating your Web presentation, you need to do some planning.

To begin designing your Web presentation, answer the following questions:

- What's the purpose of this Web presentation?
- What audience am I trying to reach and how does that affect my presentation?

- What information am I trying to convey?
- How will I organize the information?
- What should the home or top page have on it to attract visitors?

After defining the goals of your Web presentation, you should define the structure on paper; that is, draw all the pages, define all the links, and make all your decisions before you start to code.

Use the top page or home page to organize the entire site. Create a list that links to all next level pages. Use a consistent layout for each page in the presentation; that is, use the same background, the same buttons in the same location on each page, and consistent type.

A good rule to remember at this point is to include only one topic per page, keep the pages short enough so that the user doesn't have to scroll to see the entire page. Don't include a large graphic at the top of the page, which will take too long to load.

Once you know what you want to say and how you want to present it, you're ready to write the content of the presentation. When writing for online publication, you should follow the guidelines in the Web Page Design Checklist.

WEB PAGE DESIGN CHECKLIST

☑ Be brief—use lists whenever possible; use short words in short sentences

☑ Be clear—avoid vague words

☑ Use simple language—avoid extra words

☑ Check your spelling and grammar—the world can visit your site

☑ Use the following features to tie the presentation together:

  ☒ Use hypertext lists or menus

  ☒ Include a link only if it's a useful way to relevant information

  ☒ Use consistent terminology throughout the presentation

☒   Use consistent icons throughout the presentation

☒   Use the same banner or logo on each page

☒   Use consistent layout for each page of the presentation

☒   Include a way back to the home page on each page and place it in the same location on each page

☒   Make sure all links are current

☒   Include a graphic only if it relates to the content

☒   Include alternative text with every graphic

☒   Make sure each page can stand alone yet remains consistent with the rest of the site

☒   Don't overdo emphasizing or formatting text

☒   Make sure the text stands out from the background

☒   Use lines to separate sections of the page

☑   Try out the presentation in more than one browser

TRY THIS! PLAN A PERSONAL WEB PAGE

☑   Display a page in your browser. Display the source code.

☑   Find Web pages that belong to friends, instructors, or even people you don't know. Get an idea of content that you would want on your Web page.

☑   Plan a personal home page. Using the design questions in this chapter, determine the purpose, content, audience, etc. for your Web page.

☑   Create a paper design of your proposed Web site.

☑   For more information on HTML, visit the World Wide Web Consortium at http://w3.org

CHAPTER 2 ──○

BASIC HTML

UNDERSTANDING HTML TAGS

HTML (Hypertext Markup Language) is a set of codes that you use to create a document. These codes, called tags, format text, place graphics on the page, and create links.

These HTML tags follow a certain format, or syntax. Each tag begins with an opening angle bracket (<), ends with a closing angle bracket (>), and contains a command between the brackets; for example, <HTML> is the tag that designates the beginning of an HTML document.

Many of the tags are paired; that is, the first tag indicates the beginning of the command, and the second tag ends the command. The closing tag of the pair has the same syntax as the opening tag, but includes a forward slash (/) before the command. For example, the tag for the ending of an HTML document is </HTML>. All text between the opening and closing tags is affected by the tags. For example:

> <HTML>
>
> the entire Web document
>
> </HTML>

If you forget to close a paired set of tags or you include a backslash or some other character rather than a forward slash, the tag won't be closed, and the command will stay in effect.

USING HTML STRUCTURE TAGS

A Web page has two main sections: the head section and the body section. The head section must contain a title. Many browsers display this title in the title bar when the document is displayed. The body section contains the information—text, graphics, and so on—that will appear on the screen. The structure of a Web document looks like:

```
<HTML>
    <HEAD>
        <TITLE> text that appears in title bar</TITLE>
    </HEAD>
    <BODY>
        all information that will be displayed on the screen
    </BODY>
</HTML>
```

Remember these points about titles:

☑   A Web page can have only one title.

☑   The title should be specific and descriptive because it's used in a browser's history list, as bookmarks, and in indexes or other programs that catalog Web pages.

☑   The title should be concise because browsers place it in the title bar of the browser—not in the Web document.

☑   A title can't be formatted like other text—you can't change its appearance.

☑   A title can't link to other pages.

PLACING HEADINGS IN A DOCUMENT

Once you have set up the structure of the Web document, you are ready to place text on the Web page.

You can use headings to organize the body of your Web documents, much like an outline can organize a conventional document. HTML has six levels of headings, designated by the following tags:

Heading 1 <H1>...</H1>

Heading 2 <H2>...</H2>

Heading 3 <H3>...</H3>

Heading 4 <H4>...</H4>

Heading 5 <H5>...</H5>

Heading 6 <H6>...</H6>

Heading 1 is the most prominent of the headings and Heading 6 the least prominent. When you use the heading tags, you're telling each browser to format the text as a heading. Each individual browser formats each level of heading its own way, so you're simply setting up a structure for each browser to follow. You'll probably use the first three levels most often.

Because the title you place in the <TITLE> tag in the head section of the Web page is displayed only in the title bar of the browser, you should include a title for the page in the body section of the document. To make the title appear as text on the Web page, use the first-level heading to restate the title of the page, or provide a more complete title. Figure 2.1 shows a sample page with the title in the title bar and the six headings.

One new feature (supported by both Netscape Navigator 4.0 and Internet Explorer 4.0) is style sheets. This feature works just like style feature in a word processing program; that is, it applies formatting easily and allows for modifications to be made quickly. You can use the headings described above to create your own styles. For example, if you want to change the size of the H1 text to be 24 point, you would use the <STYLE> tag to redefine the H1 tag. By placing the <STYLE> tag in the <HEAD> section, you would redefine the H1 tag for the entire document. For example:

<HTML>

<HEAD>

    <TITLE> title in title bar</TITLE>

    <STYLE>

        H1 {font-size: 24pt}

    </STYLE>

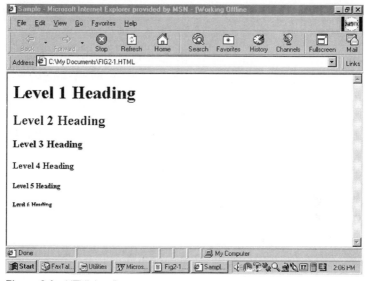

Figure 2.1   HTML headings

```
        </HEAD>
        <BODY>
                <H1> Larger heading</H1>
        </BODY>
        </HTML>
```

Notice the syntax of the <STYLE> tag:

- ☑ You place the tag you want to define right after the open <STYLE> tag
- ☑ You don't place the brackets around the tag to be redefined
- ☑ Place the new definition in curly brackets {....}
- ☑ The definition is made up of the property, followed by a colon, and the value to be assigned
- ☑ Close the <STYLE> tag

PLACING TEXT IN AN HTML DOCUMENT

You are now ready to add text to the HTML document, just as you would in any conventional document. Note that HTML doesn't recognize when you press the Enter key to end a paragraph. You need to include a <P> tag to start each new paragraph.

Each heading, <H1> through <H6>, automatically includes a paragraph break; therefore, you use the <P> tag only for new paragraphs that don't follow a heading. The end of the paragraph can include the closing paragraph tag </P>, but that's optional; however, you should get into the habit of including it for clarity and completeness. Figure 2.2 shows a sample page in Notepad. Notice the <P> tags.

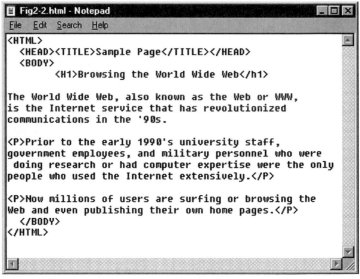

Figure 2.2   Codes using <P> tags

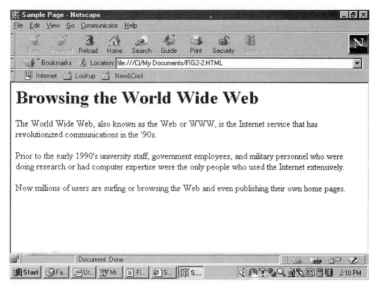

Figure 2.3   Result of <P> tags

Figure 2.3 shows the result of those codes displayed in a browser.

INSERTING LINE BREAKS

When you use the paragraph tags (<P>...</P>), browsers insert white space. Sometimes you'll want to place some text on a line by itself, without including extra white space above it. You can use the line break tag, <BR>, to place text on the next line. There is no closing tag for the line break tag. Figure 2.4 shows the sample page in Notepad. Notice the <BR> tags.

Figure 2.5 shows the results in a browser. Compare the results to Figure 2.3 that used the <P> tags.

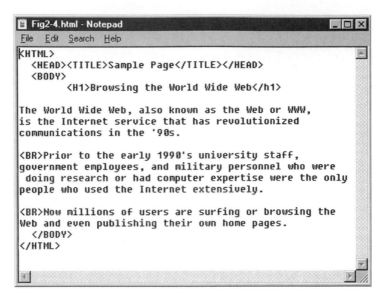

Figure 2.4   Code for <BR> tags

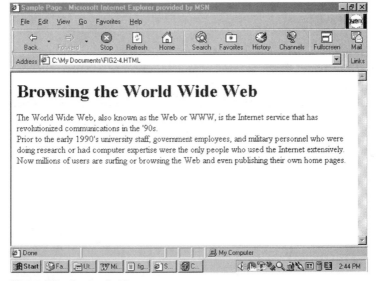

Figure 2.5   Result of <BR> tags

ENHANCING TEXT

Emphasizing text by formatting characters is common to all word processing software—you usually select the text and choose the formatting command, such as bold or italic. For the same reasons that you format characters in a word processing document, often you'll want to format text in an HTML document. The paired tags <B>...</B>, for example, make the text between the tags bold. This type of formatting is known as physical formatting in Web documents.

The appearance of Web documents is controlled by the browser software that the client uses, which may or may not be able to handle some of the very specific physical tags in your HTML document.

The second type of formatting, called logical formatting, is the more popular choice. Logical formatting is used more often than physical formatting to get around this problem of browsers not recognizing physical tag and thus not formatting the text at all. Logical formatting simply tells the browser how the text is to be used. When you use logical formatting tags to format text, you're simply telling the browser to emphasize the text, for example, rather than boldfacing it physically. That way, each browser will give the text some formatting that emphasizes that text. Table 2.1 shows the logical tags, and table 2.2 shows the physical tags.

Remember to use logical tags instead of physical tag whenever possible. Also avoid using too much formatting, making the screen hard to read. Many people avoid the blink tag totally for this reason.

Table 2.1   Logical tags

Tag	Result
<EM>....</EM>	Emphasis tag, many browsers place the text within the tags in italics.
<STRONG>...</STRONG>	Provides strong emphasis. Many browsers boldface the text with the tags.

Table 2.2 PHYSICAL TAGS

TAG	RESULT
<B>...</B>	Bolds text
<I>...</I>	Italicizes text
<CENTER>...</CENTER>	Centers text
<U>...</U>	Underlines text
<STRIKE>...</STRIKE>	Strikes through text
<BLINK>...</BLINK>	Creates blinking text
_{...}	Subscripts text—lowers the marked text below the rest of the line, as the 2 is lowered here: H_2O
^{...}	Superscripts text—raises the marked text above the rest of the line, as the 3 is raised here: [23]

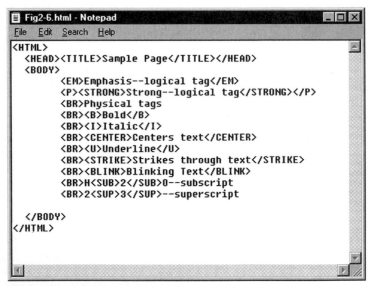

Figure 2.6 Codes for text formatting tags

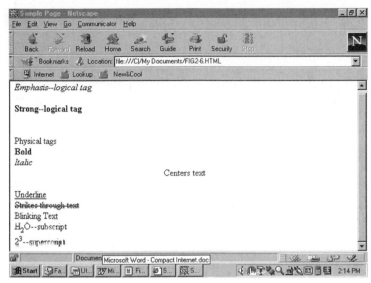

Figure 2.7   Results of formatting tags

CREATING NESTED TAGS

Sometimes you may want text to have more than one formatting tag, such as emphasizing and blinking the same text; tags combined in this way are called nested tags. If you want text in a heading to blink, for example, you would include the <BLINK> tag with the heading tag.

To make the text *Computer Textbooks* appear as a blinking Heading 1, you would write the code as follows:

<H1><BLINK>Computer Textbooks</BLINK></H1>

When you nest tags, pay careful attention to the order in which they are closed. The last tag opened must be closed first. Notice that the blink tag is closed before the Heading 1 tag in the example. This is the correct syntax.

USING ATTRIBUTES WITH TAGS

You can include attributes with tags; these attributes further define the tag. The attribute is entered after the command and before the final angle bracket. Some attributes appear by themselves, and other attributes can appear with a value modifier. The syntax of an attribute with a value modifier is as follows: attribute=value. For example, you can include the ALIGN attribute with an H1 tag to center the heading.

<H1 ALIGN=CENTER>Computer Textbooks</H1>

In this example, the text *Computer Textbooks* will appear formatted for Heading 1 because of the <H1> tag and centered because the ALIGN attribute is assigned the value CENTER.

In this example, the CENTER value is a given value; that is, you choose one value from the available ALIGN values of LEFT, RIGHT, CENTER. You can choose only one value. A given value doesn't need any other punctuation around it, such as quotation marks.

However, some commands allow you to include an attribute that has any value, for example, a number to define a size or a URL to define an address; these values need to be enclosed in straight quotation marks ("...").

CHANGING THE FONT SIZE

You can change the font size for the entire Web document, or you can change the size of a character, word, or group of words.

To change the font size for the entire document, you use the <BASEFONT> tag. This tag has a required attribute, SIZE=VALUE. You can define the value using a number from 1 to 7, where 3 is the default size, or you can use relative size changes such as +1 or −1. (Relative sizes still must fall in the range 1–7.) The <BASEFONT> tag appears as follows:

<BASEFONT SIZE=4>

or

<BASEFONT SIZE=+1>

These two examples actually call for the same font size.

You may find increasing the size of the base font useful for short Web documents to improve their appearance; for long Web documents, you can decrease the base font to fit more on the page.

To change the size of a character, word, or group of words in the Web document, you use the <FONT> tag. This tag also has a required attribute, SIZE=VALUE. You define the value using a number from 1 to 7, where 3 is the default size, or you can use relative size changes such as +1 or −1. (Relative sizes still must fall in the range 1–7.) The <FONT> tag appears as follows:

<FONT SIZE=5>text</FONT>

or

<FONT SIZE=+2>text</FONT>

Notice that the <BASEFONT> tag isn't a paired tag, but the <FONT> tag is. When you close the <FONT> command with the </FONT> tag, the font size returns to the base font setting.

Figure 2.8 shows the HTML source code for the base font set at 5 and the font size ranging from 1 to 7. Figure 2.9 shows results of font codes.

CREATING LISTS

Because the text on Web pages needs to be short and concise, placing text in lists can be helpful. The most common type of list is the unordered list (also called a bulleted list). It's a short list of information that doesn't need to be presented in any particular order. The unordered list appears with bullets (special characters)

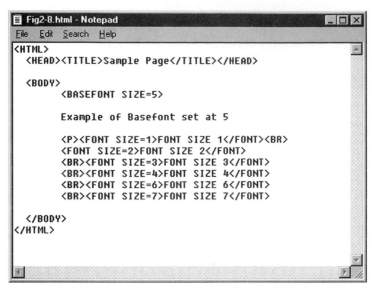

Figure 2.8 Font codes

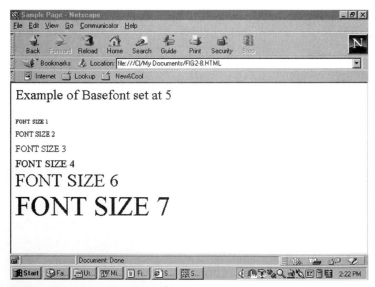

Figure 2.9 Results of font codes

before each line item. Remember these important points about unordered lists:

☑ Each list begins with the <UL> tag and ends with the </UL> tag

☑ Each line of the list must be indicated with the <LI> tag, which is not paired

☑ Each line of the unordered list appears indented and is preceded by a bullet (exact display varies from browser to browser)

Here is an example of an unordered list:

```
<UL>

        <LI>first item

        <LI>second item

        <LI>third item

</UL>
```

Sometimes the information you're presenting in a list in a Web document should show a defined sequence, such as instructions for steps in a process. You can create an ordered list (also called a numbered list). You start the list with the <OL> tag and end the list with the </OL> tag. Within those tags, begin each line you would like numbered with the <LI> tag; the ordered list is automatically numbered for you. Following is an example of an ordered list:

```
<OL>

        <LI>first item

        <LI>second item

        <LI>third item

</OL>
```

```
Fig2-10.html - Notepad
File  Edit  Search  Help
<HTML>
  <HEAD><TITLE>Sample Page</TITLE></HEAD>
  <BODY>
        <H1>An Unordered List</H1>
        <UL>
                <LI>first item
                <LI>second item
                <LI>third item
        </UL>

        <H1>An Ordered List</H1>
        <OL>
                <LI>first item
                <LI>second item
                <LI>third item
        </OL>
  </BODY>
</HTML>
```

Figure 2.10 Codes for unordered and ordered lists

TRY THIS! CREATE A WEB PAGE AND INCLUDE TEXT

☑ Using the design you created in the previous chapter, create the structure for your Web page.

☑ Include text on the Web page.

☑ Include an unordered list.

☑ Include an ordered list.

☑ Format the text.

CHAPTER 3

ENHANCING THE HOME PAGE

ADDING A HORIZONTAL LINE

You can place a horizontal line or rule across the page by including the <HR> tag at the location where you want the line to appear. The <HR> tag is not a paired tag; there is no closing tag. The <HR> tag can use the SIZE= and WIDTH= attributes to change the length and width of the line.

Lines are an effective means of dividing a page. For example, you can use a line to separate the main part of the page from footer information. Footer information should include the author or person responsible for the page, an email address, and other contact information such as a mail address or phone number. The date of the last revision of page is also usually contained in the footer. You can use the <ADDRESS>...</ADDRESS> tag to format the text (usually italic and a reduced font size), or you can format the text yourself. Figure 3.1 shows the code for a line that separates the footer information from the rest of the body, and Figure 3.2 displays the results.

```
Fig3-1.html - Notepad
File   Edit   Search   Help
<HTML>
  <HEAD><TITLE>Sample Page</TITLE></HEAD>
  <BODY>
        <H2>Sample Page with Address in Footer</H2>
        <UL>
                <LI>first item
                <LI>second item
                <LI>third item
        </UL>
        <BR>
        <BR>
        <HR>

        <P><ADDRESS>Lane Community College
        <BR>4000 E. 30<SUP>th</SUP> Ave.
        <BR>Eugene, Oregon 97405</ADDRESS>
  </BODY>
</HTML>
```

Figure 3.1   Code for a footer

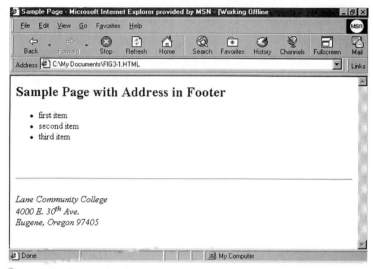

Figure 3.2   Results of code

INCLUDING GRAPHICS

Two universal formats are used for Web graphics: .GIF and .JPG. The .GIF standard, short for Graphics Interchange Format, was developed by CompuServe and is the format that displays in the greatest number of browsers. The .JPG, which stands for Joint Photographic Experts Group, is best used for images such as photographs that contain many subtle colors.

To include an image on your Web page, you use the <IMG> tag. The tag includes the SRC="filename" attribute. For example, to display a graphic named logo.gif, you enter the following:

<IMG SRC="logo.gif">

In this example, the image logo.gif will display at the location of the tag.

Including alternative text with images for users who can't or don't want to view images is also a good idea. If a user has graphic display turned off or is using a text browser, the text will display on the person's screen. This syntax for including alternative text is:

<IMG SRC="logo.gif" ALT="our company logo">

Two other attributes that you should include with every image are HEIGHT and WIDTH. If you designate a width and height for each image, your page will load into browsers much faster. The reason for this is that browsers have to calculate the width and height for every image, so by specifying the size, you avoid the calculations. The syntax for including the width and height is:

<IMG SRC="logo.gif" ALT="our company logo"
WIDTH="40" HEIGHT="200">

The images are measured in pixels, that is, picture elements. These are dots on your screen that make up the image.

Other attributes you might want to include with your image set the alignment of the image in relation to the surrounding text. The syntax is:

<IMG SRC="logo.gif" ALT="our company logo"
ALIGN=MIDDLE>

Table 3.1 defines the values used with the ALIGN attribute.

Table 3.1   VALUES USED WITH THE ALIGN ATTRIBUTE

VALUE	RESULT
MIDDLE	One line of text is placed at the middle of the image
TOP	One line of text is placed at the top of the image
BOTTOM	One line of text is placed at the bottom of the image
LEFT	The image is at the left of the screen and one or more lines of text appear to the right of the image
RIGHT	The image is at the right of the screen and one or more lines of text appear to the left of the image

You have seen how to create a bulleted list using the <UL> tag. Many people prefer to create or download bullets from clipart sites to create more impact on their Web page. Once you have a bullet you want to use, simply type the text, and include the <IMG SRC="bullet.gif"> command where you want the bullet to appear. You can use the same bullet numerous times in a list or you can use different ones.

You have also used the <HR> tag to create a separator line on a Web page. Many people also prefer to create or download color lines from clipart sites to match their bullets and create a more unified look to their pages.

Figure 3.3 shows the code for a logo, bullets, and a line, and Figure 3.4 displays the results.

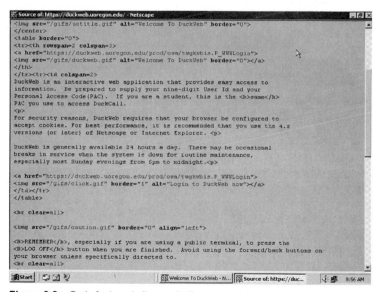

Figure 3.3   Code for logo, bullets, and a line

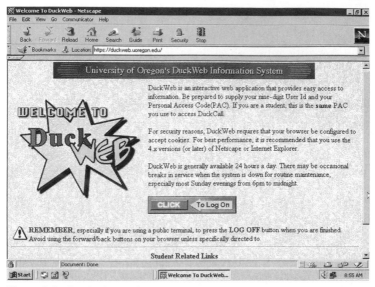

Figure 3.4   Result of the code

ADDING A BACKGROUND COLOR

When you started your Web document, you defined the opening of the body of the document with the <BODY> tag. If you want to change the background color of your Web document from the standard gray, you do so by adding the BGCOLOR attribute to the opening body tag. For example, if you want to have a blue background, here's how you do it:

<BODY BGCOLOR=#0000FF>

In this example, #0000FF is the RGB (Red, Green, Blue) value of blue; that is, its red, green, and blue values. The first two digits in this number designate the red value; the second two digits, the green value; and the last two digits, the blue value. To specify these RGB values for the color you want, you must know or look up the hexadecimal equivalent that represents the color. Table 3.2 lists some common colors you might want to use.

Table 3.2 COMMON COLORS

COLOR	HEX EQUIVALENT
Black	#000000
White	#FFFFFF
Green	#00FF00
Red	#FF0000
Tan	#DEB887
Turquoise	#19CCDF
Magenta	#FF00FF
Yellow	#FFFF00

Hexadecimal (or hex) is a numbering system that uses base 16 rather than base 10. The hex system uses the numbers 0–9 along with the letters A–F. This numbering system enables you to represent all numbers up to 256 with only two digits and has been used extensively with computers for that reason. If you aren't used to working in hex, don't be confused by the mixture of letters and numbers. Just remember that letters represent numbers greater than 9 with F being the highest.

USING A GRAPHIC AS A BACKGROUND

Instead of changing the background color, you can use an image as the background, such as the company's or organization's logo. To add an image to the background of your Web document, you use the BACKGROUND attribute with the opening <BODY> tag. The format of the BACKGROUND attribute is:

<BODY BACKGROUND="logo.gif">

If the image is small, the browser tiles or repeats the image so that it covers the document's background.

Be sure to use a light colored image that doesn't make the page difficult to read. Figure 3.5 shows a logo included as a background.

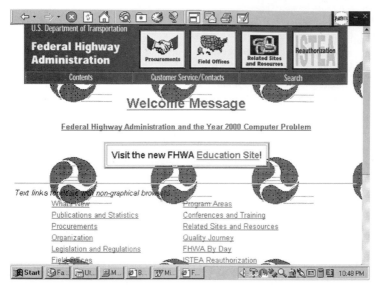

Figure 3.5 Page with a logo

CHANGING TEXT COLOR

After changing the appearance of the background of a Web document, you might also want to change the color of the text that appears on the page. You do so by adding an attribute to the opening <BODY> tag.

You can change the color of four different types of text:

☑ Change the color of the normal text that appears in the document with the TEXT attribute

☑ Change the color of links (hypertext) with the LINK attribute

☑ Change the color of visited links (links the user has clicked) using the VLINK attribute

☑ Change the color of active links with ALINK. This attribute designates the color of the link as you click it.

You use the same RGB hexadecimal equivalents described for the background colors to designate the desired colors of text. To change the body text to red, for example, you would type the following:

<BODY TEXT=#FF0000>

When you use the TEXT attribute to designate red text with the blue background, it looks like this:

<BODY BGCOLOR=#0000FF TEXT=#FF0000>

This command designates the LINK value as pink and the VLINK as green.

<BODY BGCOLOR=#0000FF TEXT=#FF0000
LINK=#F33E96 VLINK=#00FF7F>

INSERTING SPECIAL CHARACTERS

HTML documents are ASCII text files; that is, they are files based on the American Standard Code for Information Interchange (ASCII). ASCII files use only the letters, numbers, and symbols that you can type from your keyboard, which, along with some essential control characters, equals 128 characters. Just as you might include special characters not on the keyboard in a word processing document, you can also include special characters in a Web document. Most word processing software enables you to select the character in a dialog box and insert it into the document. However, to insert special characters using HTML, you need to do so manually—by typing the name or number of the special character.

You can use two methods to include a character from the extended ASCII. If the special character has a name, you can use the name; otherwise, you need to use the character's number, which is designated by its location in the character set. Whether you use the character's name or number, you must start the code with an ampersand (&) and close it with a semicolon (;). The number sign appears immediately after the ampersand in codes using numbers. Table 3.3 shows the syntax for some commonly used special characters.

Table 3.3 COMMONLY USED SPECIAL CHARACTERS

CHARACTER	NAME	CODE
"	&copy;	&copy;
"	&reg;	&#174;
È	&Egrave;	&#200;
¥	&yen;	&#165;
£	&pound;	&#163;
>	&gt;	&#62;
<	&lt;	&#60;
&	&amp;	&#38;

Notice that the table includes some characters that are located on your keyboard. These special characters present a problem in HTML because of the syntax of the language. For example, to type A < B, you need to designate the less-than sign (<) as a special character because a browser knows that the less-than sign starts all HTML tags. The same holds true for other HTML characters.

INCLUDING TABLES

Tables are often used in Web page development to display information because you can organize bodies of information so that the reader can quickly see the overall picture.

Tables are made up of data arranged in columns (vertically) and rows (horizontally). The intersection of a column and row is known as a cell; data is placed in cells. Tables can also be used as a design element in HTML. You will find that many people use tables to have control of the elements on the screen.

The entire contents of the table are contained between the opening and closing <TABLE> tags.

<TABLE>

entire contents of table

</TABLE>

The table is defined row by row; that is, you define the contents of the first row and then the contents of each subsequent row. You start each row with the <TR> tag, which stands for table row, and end each row with the </TR> tag. Everything between those two tags will appear in one row of the table. The syntax is

<TABLE>

<TR>

text in the first row

</TR>

<TR>

text in the second row

</TR>

<TR>

text in the third row

</TR>

</TABLE>

You then define the contents of each cell in each row:

The <TH> tag, table header, is used to bold cell contents, and the <TD> tag, table data, is used for unformatted cells. Both tags are paired tags.

For example, if the first row of a three-column, three-row table contains headings and the rest of the table contains data, this is how the coding looks.

<TABLE>

<TR>

<TH>heading </TH>

<TH>heading </TH>

<TH>heading </TH>

```
                    </TR>

                    <TR>

              <TD>data</TD>

              <TD>data</TD>

              <TD>data</TD>

                    </TR>

                    <TR>

              <TD>data</TD>

              <TD>data</TD>

              <TD>data</TD>

                    </TR>

                 </TABLE>
```

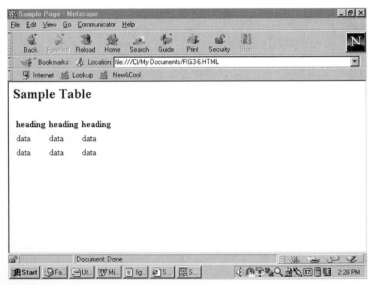

Figure 3.6   Sample table

To set a table off from the rest of the Web document, you can add the BORDER attribute to the opening <TABLE> tag. The BORDER attribute places a border with a width of 1 pixel around the outside edge of the table and also places borders around each individual cell. The syntax for the BORDER attribute is:

<TABLE BORDER>

To change the width of the outside border, you can add a value to the BORDER attribute. The value is the number of pixels that will appear around the outside edge of the table. To increase the border to a width of 4 pixels, for example, use the format:

<TABLE BORDER=4>

To change the spacing between cells so that the data is easier to read, you can add the CELLSPACING attribute to the opening <TABLE> tag, along with a value in pixels. The default cell spacing is 2 pixels. The following command assigns a value of 8 pixels:

<TABLE CELLSPACING=8>

To add space around the cell contents, you use the CELL-PADDING attribute along with a value in pixels. The default cell padding is 1 pixel. This command sets the cell padding at 6 pixels:

<TABLE CELLPADDING=6>

TRY THIS! ENHANCE YOUR WEB PAGE

Enhance your Web page by including the following:

- ☑ Include a line using the <HR> tag
- ☑ Include a line that you download from a clipart site
- ☑ Include a graphic on the page
- ☑ Include a list with bullets that you download from a clipart site

☑ Change the color of the background or include an image on the background

☑ Place some information in a table

☑ Include a footer that uses the <ADDRESS> tag and includes the copyright symbol

LINKING TO OTHER DOCUMENTS AND CREATING FORMS

INSERTING LINKS

One feature that makes Web documents so powerful is their linking capability. A link provides text or an object that the user can click, and the user's display automatically "jumps" to the new document. The link can be a location within the same document or to a different Web document.

To create a link, use the <A> tag—anchor tag. You set the opening and closing <A> tags around the text that you want the user to click to view another document. The <A>tag must contain the URL (Uniform Resource Locator) for the desired document. The syntax is as follows:

<A HREF="URL">text user clicks</A>

A more complete URL would look like the following:

<A HREF="http://web.site.com/path/document.html">text user clicks</A>

For example,

<A HREF="prenhall.com">Prentice Hall</A>

The text located between the opening and closing <A> tags appears in the browser as hypertext. When the user clicks the hypertext, he is transferred to the Web document defined in the URL by the Hypertext Reference (HREF).

You may have seen Web pages that have phrases such as *click here* to indicate a link. You should avoid meaningless text and instead create links that flow with the text. The user knows to click the text without having to be told to click there, because the text has been formatted as hypertext—usually blue and underlined. Figure 4.1 shows the code for a page with several links, and Figure 4.2 shows the result in the browser.

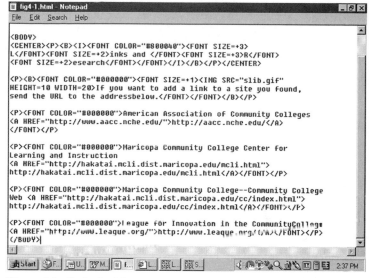

Figure 4.1   Codes for links

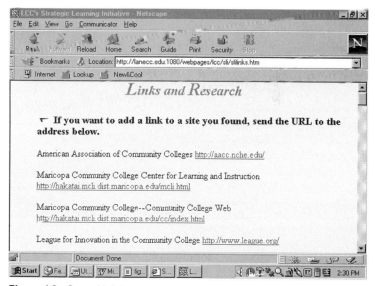

Figure 4.2   Page with links

LINKING WITHIN THE SAME DOCUMENT

Linking to a different location in the same document is a lot like placing a bookmark in a word processing document, because you must name the location where you want the link to go when the user clicks the hypertext. For example, if you want the user to go to a section that provides help, you go to that section and place the following anchor tag:

<A NAME="help">Help Section</A>

This tag names the section of the document *help*, starting with the text *Help Section*.

After naming a location in the document, you place the anchor tag around the text that you want the user to click. For example, if you want the user to click on the text, *For help on this topic,* you would place the following anchor tag and Hypertext reference:

<A HREF="#help">For help on this topic</A>

When the user wants help, he can click on the text *For help on this topic,* and he will be transferred to the Help Section of the document. Including a link back to the original location for the user is also common courtesy on the Web. So you give the original location a name such as top and include the anchor tags to return the user to the top of the document.

Notice that when linking to another document, the Hypertext Reference in the opening <A> tag contains the complete URL of the document. When linking to another location in the same document, the Hypertext Reference in the opening <A> tag contains a # followed by the name of the anchor that you set.

USING GRAPHICS AND BUTTONS AS LINKS

You can create buttons using a graphics program such as PaintShop Pro, which is an excellent shareware program. You can also find numerous clipart buttons on the Web. You will want your user to be able to click the button and return to the home page, return to the top, get more information, or be transferred to another page. To make a button a link, you use the anchor tag in the same way you used it in the previous section to create hypertext. That is, you place the anchor tags around the IMG tag. This syntax can also be used to for any image on your Web page. For example, a small, thumbnail image can be loaded quickly, and if you place anchor tags around the image, it can be used to click to the full-size graphic.

By placing the IMG tag within the anchor tags, the pointer will change to a hand when the user points to the image, indicating that the image is a link.

A button or icon can be used to link the user to another page. The Hunger Site, which helps fight world hunger, has the user click a button to donate food. When you click the Donate Free Food button, you are connected to a page detailing which sponsors have paid for your donation. Many people make the Hunger Site their home page and click the button every day. See Figure 4.3 below.

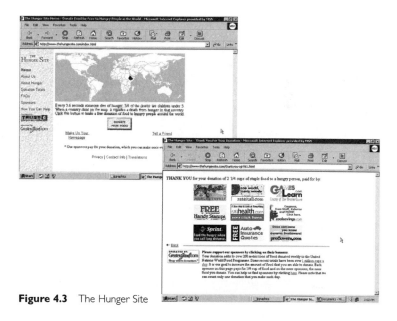

Figure 4.3 The Hunger Site

CREATING AN EMAIL LINK

You will want to create an easy way for people who visit your Web site to get in touch with you. One simple way is to create an e-mail button. When the user clicks the button, a pre-addressed e-mail form displays.

This type of link is called a mail to link because the reserved word mailto will precede your email address in the Hypertext Reference.

The following examples show a mail button and text for the user to click.

```
          <A HREF="mailto:sue@efn.com">
SRC="mail_button.gif"> </A>
```

```
 <A HREF="mailto:jim@telnet.org">Email Jim Smith</A>
```

Figure 4.4 shows the result of this code.

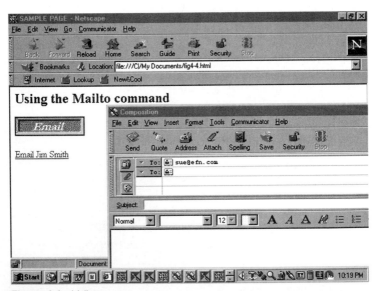

Figure 4.4   Mailto

CREATING A FORM

Forms provide the capacity to get input from visitors by allowing them to enter information into blank areas and make selections from options. This type of interaction with visitors to your Web site is a powerful feature.

A form is created in the Web document between the opening and closing <BODY> tags, and the entire body of the form is contained between the opening and closing <FORM> tags. The ACTION attribute is mandatory because it specifies the URL where data from the form is to be sent. The action here is simply to mail to an e-mail address. The METHOD attribute has only two possible values: GET and POST. When you use GET, the default value, the data is added to the end of the URL and sent to the server as a variable. POST sends a separate stream of data to the server and is used to send the information on the form to an e-mail address.

When the visitor fills out a form, the information will be sent to the owner of the page at the e-mail address specified by the ACTION attribute. For example,

```
<FORM ACTION="mailto:lindae@uoregon.edu"
METHOD=POST>
```

contents of the form

```
</FORM>
```

There are no spaces allowed in the ACTION section of the FORM tag.

After setting up the opening and closing <FORM> tags in your document, you are ready to define the user-input fields (data elements) that will appear on the form. Form fields are the same as fields used in database software or in the address file for a mail merge. That is, they're the individual elements that make up the data for one person—for example, *Last Name* might be one field, and *City* another field.

You receive input from the user with the <INPUT> tag. You need to specify the type of input by the TYPE attribute. The most

Table 4.1   ATTRIBUTES

ATTRIBUTE	DESCRIPTION
SIZE	Defines the size of the text input box on your form, in number of characters. The default setting is 20 characters.
MAXLENGTH	Defines the number of characters that will be accepted (because the user can actually type more characters than the size of the box).
NAME	Gives the text input box a data element name that identifies the information.

common type of input is TEXT. This is the format for the <IN-PUT> tag:

<INPUT TYPE="TEXT">

This HTML tag places a text input box on the form for the user to type a response to you. You can further define the text input with attributes. Table 4.1 lists the attributes.

The following example sets the size of the input box as 30 characters, with a maximum input of 40 characters from the user. The name of the box is *username*:

Enter Your Name:

<INPUT TYPE="TEXT" SIZE="30" MAXLENGTH="40" NAME="username">

Figure 4.5 shows the result of this command.

You can make your form easier to use by providing radio buttons for selecting one option from a group of options. You also can provide check boxes for selecting one or more options in a group.

To create radio buttons, specify the <INPUT> type as RADIO. You must provide a NAME attribute for the group of radio buttons—for example, using the word Amount as the name for a group of donation options.

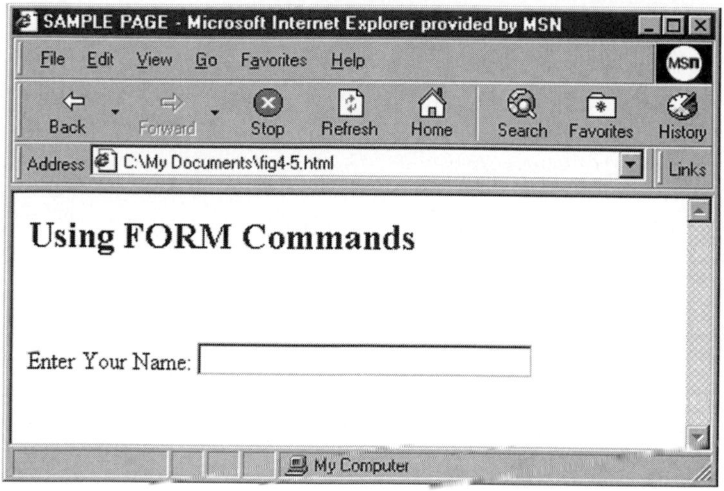

Figure 4.5   Text box

After specifying the name of the group of buttons, you must specify the individual buttons contained within the group by using the VALUE option. Whereas the group name stays the same for the group of buttons, the value for each individual button is unique. The text following the closing angle bracket (>) appears on-screen after the button explaining the button choice to the user. For example,

```
<INPUT TYPE="RADIO" NAME="CITY"
VALUE="Boston">Boston

<INPUT TYPE="RADIO" NAME="CITY"
VALUE="Cambridge">Cambridge
```

With radio buttons, the user can choose only one of the radio button options in any set or group.

Figure 4.6 shows the result of the code.

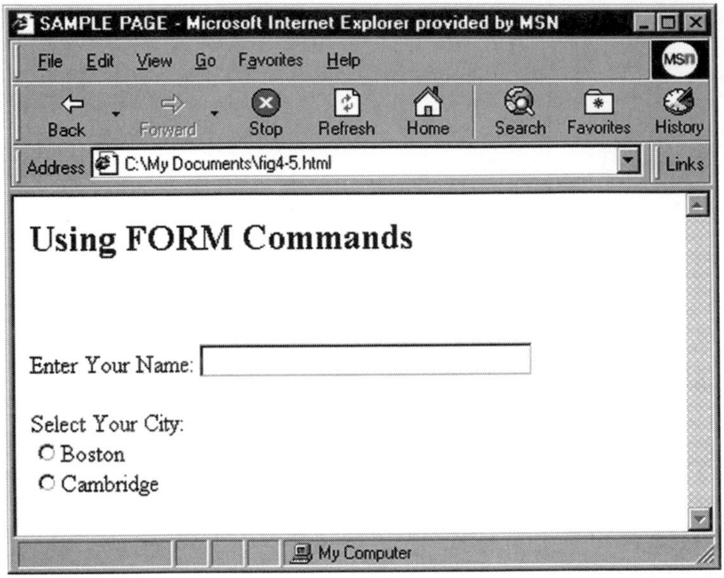

Figure 4.6   Radio buttons

The only difference between radio buttons and check boxes is that the user can make multiple selections in a set of check boxes. The procedure for creating check boxes is similar to the one for creating radio boxes. To create check boxes, you use the CHECK-BOX attribute with the <INPUT>. You can have a single check box for the user to select one option, or you can provide a group of check boxes. Check boxes are also grouped together using the same NAME attribute, and you define the value for the check box with the VALUE attribute. An example of a single check box is:

<INPUT TYPE="CHECKBOX" VALUE="information">
Please send information

An example of a set of grouped checkboxes is:

<INPUT TYPE="CHECKBOX" NAME="animal"
VALUE="panda">Giant Pandas

```
<INPUT TYPE="CHECKBOX" NAME="animal"
VALUE="turtle">Sea Turtles<BR>
```

```
<INPUT TYPE="CHECKBOX" NAME="animal"
VALUE="crane">Sandhill Cranes<BR>
```

```
<INPUT TYPE="CHECKBOX" NAME="animal"
VALUE="tiger">Tigers<BR>
```

```
<INPUT TYPE="CHECKBOX" NAME="animal"
VALUE="whale">Blue Whales
```

Figure 4.7 shows the result of the above code.

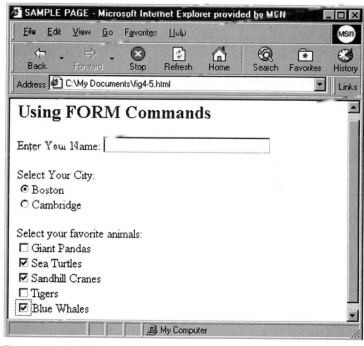

Figure 4.7 Check boxes

You can provide the user with several options by creating a list box and placing the options in the list for the user to select. You use the opening and closing <SELECT> tags to enclose the list options. Each item on the list is then identified with the <OP-TION> tag. In the following example, a list named County will be displayed, with the options Franklin, Lane, and Jefferson.

<SELECT NAME="County">

<OPTION>Franklin

<OPTION>Lane

<OPTION>Jefferson

</SELECT>

Figure 4.8 shows the result of this code.

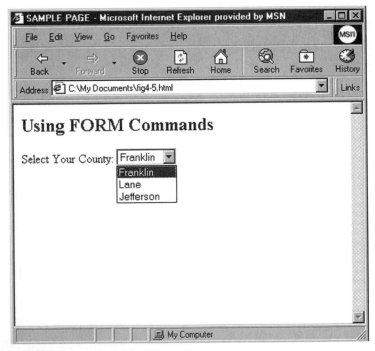

Figure 4.8   Drop-down list

If you want the user to be able to input a large amount of text, create a text area on the form with the <TEXTAREA> tag. As with other text fields, you can use the NAME attribute to define the <TEXTAREA> data, and you can also define the size of the area. The default size of the text area is 40 characters wide by 4 rows long. To change the size from the default, use the COLS and ROWS attributes:

<TEXTAREA NAME="response" COLS="20" ROWS="10">

</TEXTAREA>

Figure 4.9 shows the result of this code.

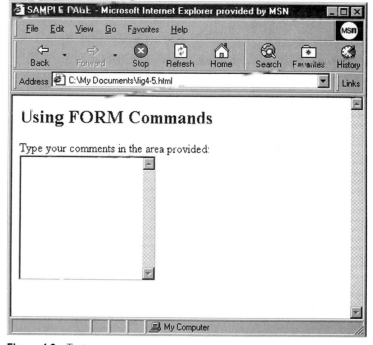

Figure 4.9 Text area

The standard way for a user to send information on a form to the server is to use a Submit button. When the user clicks the Submit button, the form contents are sent to the URL defined in the ACTION attribute of the opening <FORM> tag. The submit button's VALUE attribute allows you to define the text that appears on the button. If you don't include the VALUE attribute, the text *Submit Query* will appear on the button. This is the format:

<INPUT TYPE="SUBMIT" VALUE="Send Data">

When you include a Submit button on a form, you should also include a Reset button. The Reset button clears any fields in which the user has specified information and resets all the form's default

Figure 4.10   Submit and Reset buttons

settings. You can also use the VALUE option to change the text on the Reset button. The default text is *Reset*. This command creates a Reset button with the text *Clear* on it:

<INPUT TYPE="RESET" VALUE="Clear">

Figure 4.10 show the result of this code.

TRY THIS! LINK YOUR DOCUMENTS TO OTHERS

Make your Web site interactive by including the following:

- ☑ Links to other documents
- ☑ Links to other locations on the World Wide Web
- ☑ Links within the document
- ☑ Buttons that link to other documents
- ☑ An email link to your email address
- ☑ A form to receive information back from your visitors

CHAPTER 5 ———○

ENHANCING AND EVALUATING A HOME PAGE

USING FRAMES

Frames allow you to divide the screen display into sections. Each section then has a separate HTML file loaded into it.

You create the files loaded into the frames just as you would any HTML file. However, you must create a different type of HTML file to divide the screen and to load the files. Instead of containing a body section that uses the opening and closing <BODY> tags, you use the opening and closing <FRAMESET> tag to define the number and size of the frames. For example,

<FRAMESET cols="20%, 80%">

contents of frame

</FRAMESET>

This tag defines a screen divided into two vertical sections. The section on the left will take up 20% of the display, and the section on the right will take up 80% of the display.

To divide the screen into three horizontal bands, you would use the following:

<FRAMESET rows="30%, 40%, *">

contents of frame

</FRAMESET>

The asterisk * is used to tell the browser to use up the rest of the available display. It is also possible to define the number of pixels for each section; however, it is not recommended because of the difference in resolution from one display to another. Figure 5.1 shows a whimsical use of the frames command to construct faces randomly.

You can also combine horizontal and vertical frames so that you have both horizontal and vertical sections on the same display. However, keep your display simple—don't include too many frames so that the user sees only a small portion of several documents.

After you establish the number and size of the frames, you use the <FRAME> tag to set up the contents of each frame. The <FRAME> tag has several attributes, defined in Table 5.1.

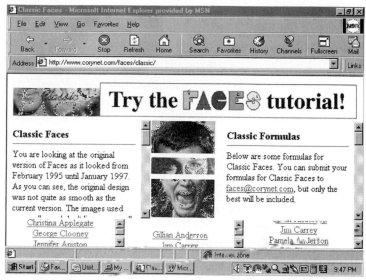

Figure 5.1 Faces game

Table 5.1 <FRAME> attributes

ATTRIBUTE	RESULT
SRC="file.html"	Places the file in the frame.
scrolling="yes/no/auto"	If scrolling equals yes, then the frame will have a scrollbar. If scrolling equals no, then the frame will not have a scroll bar. If scrolling equals auto, then if the browser determines that a scrollbar is needed, then one will be included.
NAME="name"	Will give the frame the name contained in quotation marks.
NORESIZE	Will keep the user from being able to re-size the frame.

In order to include information for users who do not have browsers capable of displaying frames, it is a common practice to use the opening and closing <NOFRAMES> tags to include information for the user. For example,

<NOFRAMES>This document can only be viewed by a browser capable of displaying frames.</NOFRAMES>

The <NOFRAMES> tag is ignored by browsers that display frames.

You can allow the user to click in one frame and load the file in another frame, as this Faces game demonstrates in Figure 5.2.

For example, you can use the frame's feature to create a menu that will stay on the screen at all times. When the user clicks a menu choice in one frame, the file is loaded into another frame. For example, in Figure 5.3 the right frame displays the menu.

In order to load the .html file in another frame, you need to include the TARGET attribute with the <A HREF> tag, making the target location the name of the frame defined in the <FRAME> tag.

Figure 5.2   Faces

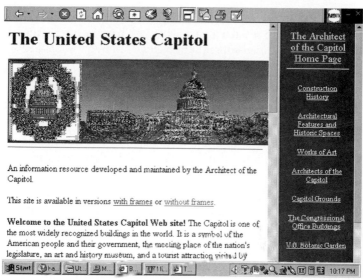

Figure 5.3 US Capitol

```
<A HREF="ocean.html" TARGET="main">the ocean</A>
```

When the visitor clicks on the text, *the ocean*, which is contained in the menu frame, the file ocean.html will load into the frame named main.

APPLYING NAVIGATION RULES

The main navigation rule for Web design is to let the user know where he is at all times and help him to proceed to the information he is looking for. Nothing is more frustrating than to land on a site and not be able to navigate it because the developer assumed everyone would visit his site starting from the top of the site.

Another navigational tip is to avoid useless clicking and page loads. Clicking through two or three extra levels that aren't necessary will turn visitors away.

Use the top page to grab the user's attention and explain what the site contains. Using an attractive list of links to other sections of the document will help load the page faster and allow the visitor to your site to see at a glance what you have to offer. This will entice visitors to load subsequent pages.

Place the most important information first because many visitors will not go past your first page.

If your site is large, think about including Next and Previous buttons on every page to direct visitors through the site.

Place all your links in one location so that you don't lose your visitor to a more interesting link in the middle of viewing your top page.

Do not place under construction signs on Web pages. Visitors get very frustrated waiting for a page to load to find out that there's nothing there.

Remember to do your planning first before you even start to code. Plan for the Web—don't just take a paper document and put it on a Web page with lots of bells and whistles. You should think about the way a user will navigate your site. Plan to present them the information they are looking for.

Don't let information or links get out-of-date. The site must always be current.

Let the visitor know what is new so that a repeat visitor will have a reason to return to your site and to stay. Give visitors reasons to bookmark your site by providing valuable information.

Include dates on the page to show updated information.

Always include a way back to the top of the presentation.

Never allow a page to be a dead end; that is, there is no way for the user to go anyplace.

FORMATTING GUIDELINES

Have a consistent theme or include unifying elements throughout the entire site by using colors, bullets, buttons, and fonts that match or complement each other. Place the logo in the same place on every page so the visitor knows where he is. Check out the feel of site—a busy or black background with dungeon and dragon art probably doesn't lend itself to a business site. Format the site for the type of information you are including and remember your audience.

Too many frames, too much animation, blinking text, text of too many sizes and colors, and large images are all a nightmare when used excessively. Even too much text will turn away visitors. Remember that simple is the best. Simple pages load fast, and users can see at a glance if the site is relevant to them. Text can be divided with lines, formatted with lists that include links to more detailed information.

USING GRAPHICS EFFECTIVELY

Remember that not all graphics on the Web are free; many are the work of artists who copyright those images and make their living from their art. Always read the copyright notice at any graphics site and adhere to the request of the site owner. If they want credit on your page, a link to their page, an email to negotiate price, or whatever, you need to adhere to their demands.

Remember that you can easily scan logos, photographs, or your own art to include on your site.

One tip is to use the same graphic, such as the company logo, on every page because most browsers store images in a cache. This will enable the browser to load the graphic file from the cache rather than having to download it, speeding up your pages.

Remember to include images only if they are relevant to the content and are an important part of the page design.

EVALUATING THE OVERALL IMPACT OF THE WEB PAGE

Have you included too many frames, as shown in Figure 5.4?

Have you included too much unformatted text, such as the page shown in Figure 5.5?

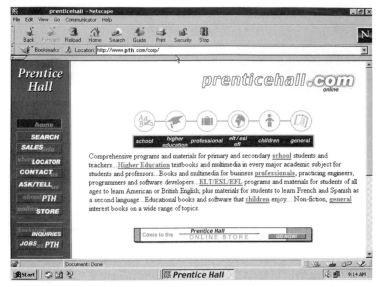

Figure 5.4   A page with too many frames

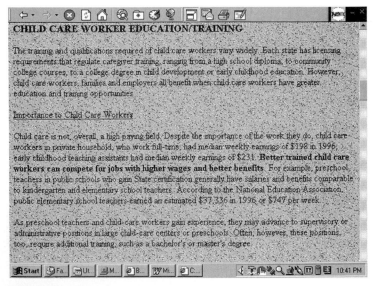

Figure 5.5   Text

Figure 5.6 PBS

Does the top page invite visitors in and grab their attention by clearly showing them what you have to offer? Figure 5.6 shows a top page that has impact.

Post your site locally and get feedback from friends and colleagues. Take their advice and spend time making your Web site user friendly.

PUBLISHING YOUR WEB PAGE

After your web document is easy to navigate, fast to load, free of grammar and spelling errors, all content is accurate, and you have checked it out in several browsers, you're ready to publish it. Some people think that others can access their document because it's on their computer's hard drive and they are linked to the World Wide Web. This is not the case; you have to place your Web documents along with any graphic files on a Web server. If you have an Internet Service Provider, you should check to see what kind of services they offer. Do they impose any types of limits? Do they support all the features that you want? What do they charge? If you're designing a commercial site, you might explore maintaining your own Web server so that you have more control over security and management of the site.

You can search the Web for services that host Web sites to find the one that best suites your needs.

In order to transfer your Web presentation from your computer to your Web host, you will need to use FTP-File Transfer Protocol. Two common shareware FTP software packages are CUTE FTP and WS-FTP. Both are easy to use. Your Web host will supply you with the necessary information such as the Hostname, URL, and Login name.

After you publish your site, you need to help people find it. The first step is to register your site with the major search engines. However, before doing this, you should include META tags in the <HEAD> section of the top page. This can help insure that your page is indexed and described properly. You use the <META> tag to list keywords found in the document and to create a description of the Web site. With these tags, when search engines, which use spiders or robots, index your site, they will use the text and description you placed in the <META> tag.

To create a description of your site, use the "description" attribute, and to create a list of keywords, use the "keywords" attribute, and then list the keywords separated by commas. Here's an example of the <META> tag for a technical writer's site:

```
<HEAD>
    <TITLE>Cyber-Writer.com</TITLE>
    <META name="description" content="Author
of computer text books, online help systems, Web pages, and
other technical documents">
    <META name="keywords"
```

content="computer books, technical writing, textbooks, online help, editing, technical editing, Web development">
   </HEAD>

After you have included the <META> tags, you are ready to register your site with the search engines. Some of the major search engines are: Yahoo! AltaVista, Lycos, Excite, Infoseek, and WebCrawler.

Also use the URL of your site on your business cards, stationery, and other business documents.

After you've published your Web presentation, keep it maintained and up-to-date. Periodically check all links to make sure that they are still active, and add new updated information to your page so that you will have repeat visitors.

TRY THIS! IMPROVE YOUR WEB PAGE

Improve your Web page by:

☑ Including <META> tags in the <HEAD> section

☑ Testing your site on friends

☑ Checking for all spelling and grammar errors

☑ Researching Web host

☑ Finding out about FTP software

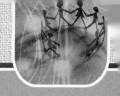

ADDING JAVASCRIPTS TO A WEB PAGE

GETTING STARTED WITH JAVASCRIPT

JavaScript is a programming or scripting language that can add interactivity to your Web site by responding to actions performed by the person viewing your document. Scripting languages allow nonprogrammers to write programs by defining the list of actions that should occur. Some examples of JavaScript scripts include: displaying messages to the user that appear on the Web page, in an alert box, or in the status line; displaying browser information, including the type of browser and plug-ins available; validating form information; creating animation; creating clocks and calendars; and, in general, performing actions in response to the user.

Sometimes people confuse JavaScript with the programming language Java. JavaScript is a simple scripting language designed to work with your browser. The script you write is placed right in the Web document, and the JavaScript code is interpreted by a browser. Java is a more complex language to program and requires a compiler to translate the program.

Netscape Communications Corporation developed JavaScript for use on Web pages, so JavaScript programs are most often run from within browser software. However, unlike HTML, JavaScript programs can encounter compatibility problems between browsers. Most problems can be avoided by using basic JavaScript features that have cross-platform support, by hiding JavaScript scripts from older browsers (as you will see later in this section), or by writing a script that detects which browser the user is running and then displays Web pages based on that information.

Since JavaScript programs can be typed right into your HTML document, you can use the tools with which you are already familiar. A JavaScript program can be placed in different locations in the HTML document depending on the job you want it to do:

- Type the script in the <HEAD> section of the page when you do not want the actions performed as the Web page is displayed by a browser but instead run in response to user actions.

- Type the script in the <BODY> section of the page when you want the actions performed as the Web page is displayed by a browser.
- Type the script inside an HTML tag to respond to actions performed by the user (called an event handler), such as when the user points the mouse over a link.
- Create a library of JavaScript scripts that are stored externally from the HTML document. The library must have a .js extension, and the document must reside on a server.

When typing a JavaScript program into the <HEAD> or <BODY> sections of the HTML document, you must place the entire script within the opening and closing <SCRIPT> tags.

```
<HTML>
<HEAD> <TITLE>page title</TITLE>
<SCRIPT>
a JavaScript script in the HEAD section is typed here
</SCRIPT>
<BODY>
<H1>page heading</H1>
<SCRIPT>
a JavaScript script in the BODY section is typed here
</SCRIPT>
</BODY>
</HTML>
```

Here's how this works. When you type a URL for a desired Web page, your browser sends an HTTP request to the server that contains the URL you requested. The server sends the Web page located at that URL to your system. Your browser scans the document for the <SCRIPT> tag, which tells the browser that the

HTML document contains a program. If the <SCRIPT> tag is located in the <HEAD> section, the JavaScript script is ignored as the page is loaded. If the <SCRIPT> tag is located in the <BODY> section, the JavaScript script will run as the page is loaded. If the JavaScript is an event handler, the script will run only when the event that triggers it occurs.

The <SCRIPT> tag includes optional attributes including the LANGUAGE attribute and the SRC attribute. You should always use the LANGUAGE attribute with the <SCRIPT> tag because it tells the browser displaying the Web page which scripting language was used to create the program. As more scripting languages are developed, browsers will need to be informed of the language used. For example, you would type the following:

```
<SCRIPT LANGUAGE="JavaScript">
a JavaScript script is typed here
</SCRIPT>
```

The LANGUAGE attribute can further specify the version of JavaScript so that older versions of the language won't attempt to run the program. To limit use to Netscape 4.0 and above, you would specify JavaScript 1.2 by typing the following:

```
<SCRIPT LANGUAGE="JavaScript1.2">
a JavaScript script is typed here
</SCRIPT>
```

A second optional attribute, SRC, is used to access an external JavaScript library file by specifying its URL. For example, for a file named library.js located at mysite.com, you would type the following:

```
<SCRIPT LANGUAGE="JavaScript"
SRC="http://www.mysite.com/library.js">
</SCRIPT>
```

When older browsers encounter the <SCRIPT> tag, errors can result because they try to display the codes as HTML. One method used by programmers to keep older browsers from displaying error messages is to hide the actual script by placing the entire JavaScript script inside an HTML Comment tag. Remember that the HTML opening Comment tag <!— and the closing Comment tag —> enclose text that will be ignored by the browser. In this case, browsers that can't display the JavaScript program will ignore it instead of trying to display it as regular HTML. For example, you would type the following:

```
<SCRIPT LANGUAGE="JavaScript">

<!—HIDE THE SCRIPT FROM OLDER BROWSERS

the JavaScript script is typed here

// END OF THE COMMENT—>

</SCRIPT>
```

Notice the two forward slashes (//) in the example that appear on the line that contains the text *END OF THE COMMENT*. To place a comment within a JavaScript script, you must start the line with two forward slashes (//). It is a good idea to place comments in your JavaScript scripts so that you will be able to remember what the script is supposed to do or to allow others to understand your script.

You can also use the <NOSCRIPT> tag that allows you to place alternative text on the screen for browsers that can't run the script. For example, text you place between the opening and closing <NOSCRIPT> tags will be displayed on the Web page. However, the <NOSCRIPT> tag is ignored if the script can be run. For example, you would type the following:

```
<SCRIPT LANGUAGE="JavaScript">

<!—HIDE THE SCRIPT FROM OLDER BROWSERS

the JavaScript script is typed here

// END OF THE COMMENT—>

</SCRIPT>
```

```
<NOSCRIPT>
```

Your browser can't display the results of the JavaScript
```
<BR>
```
Download a newer browser.
```
</NOSCRIPT>
```

BECOMING FAMILIAR WITH JAVASCRIPT

JavaScript is a simple example of object-oriented programming languages. In object-oriented programming, information is organized by objects that have certain characteristics and can be acted upon. JavaScript includes many built-in objects, and you can also create your own. For example, a Window is a built-in JavaScript object. Further, an object has properties that describe it. Moreover, a Window object includes a document property that is the HTML document displayed in the window and the status property that is text appearing in the status bar. The syntax for writing an object with its property is designated from left to right, that is, starting with the object first and separating it from the property with a period (object.property). For instance, to access the status bar of a window, you would type the following:

window.status

An object also has methods that describe what the object can do. For example, a Window object can open other windows; it can come into focus, meaning that a window behind another window moves to the front, or it can be blurred, meaning that a window is moved out of focus or behind other windows. The syntax for writing an object with its method is designated from left to right, that is, starting with the object first and separating it from the method with a period (object.method ()). For instance, to open a window, you would type the following:

window.open ()

Two parentheses must always be typed immediately following the method. If no further information is needed, the parentheses will remain empty.

Further, in JavaScript properties of objects can also be objects themselves. For example, the Window object discussed previously included the document property that is the actual HTML document displayed in the window. The document property is also an object that has properties. In order for this system to work so that it is clear what is an object, property, or method, JavaScript makes use of a hierarchy of objects called the Document Object Model, or DOM. This hierarchy starts with the largest built-in object and works down. For example, if a window contains a document that contains a form with text, a submit button, radio buttons, and check boxes, the hierarchy would look like the following diagram:

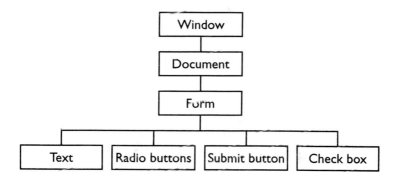

This diagram is only a small portion of the DOM. For more information on the JavaScript Document Object Model, visit the Netscape site at http://www.netscape.com.

Another aspect of JavaScript programs is events, which are actions performed by the user that trigger other actions. For example, the user might point to a graphic, type text in a form, or click on a button. You can write scripts that detect when an event happens and then respond to the event; these are called event han-

Table 6.1 Event Handlers

Event Handler	Objects	Description
onClick	Button, checkbox, radio button, hypertext link, submit button, reset button	The user clicks on one of the objects.
onLoad	Document, graphic, window	A page or image is loaded into the browser.
onMouseOver	Hyperlink, image map	The user moves the mouse over a link.
onMouseOut	Hyperlink, image map	The user moves the mouse off the link.

dlers. Event handlers are placed inside HTML tags like attributes. The syntax is typed as follows:

<HTML tag with attributes
eventHandler="action">

For example, you will use the following event handler in the next section.

<INPUT type="button" value="Open the Page"
onClick="window.open('http://www.goducks.com')">

Event handlers follow a standard syntax: the first word, such as on, is always in lowercase; each word in the event name is capitalized, such as on Click; and the entire event handler contains no spaces. Table 6.1 lists several useful event handlers and their associated objects.

WRITING SIMPLE SCRIPTS

A simple JavaScript program that you can include on your Web page opens an alert box and places the text you designate in the dialog box. You might use an alert box to feature sale items on a commercial site, as shown in Figure 6.1.

Figure 6.1 An alert box

You could call the alert box by typing the following code in the body of the document:

```
<SCRIPT LANGUAGE="JavaScript">
<!—Hide from old browsers
//places an alert box on the screen
        window.alert("50% off selected items");
//end of the comment—>
</SCRIPT>
```

However, because Window is the default top-level object, you don't need to type it in the script. You can simply type the line as follows:

```
alert("50% off selected items");
```

Notice two important syntax elements of this script:

1. The text that appears in the alert box is placed within quotation marks inside the parentheses.
2. The JavaScript statement ends with a semicolon. The semicolon is used as the end punctuation for all JavaScript statements.

The hierarchy for this script is that the default top-level object window uses the method alert with a prompt.

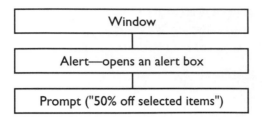

You can create a second script that also places text on a Web page by using the command document.write ("text that will appear in the document"). Whatever appears inside the parentheses will be written to the document. The following script gets the date that the document was last modified from the server and writes it on the Web page, as shown in Figure 6.2.

You would type the following in the BODY:

```
<P>This page was last modified:
<SCRIPT LANGUAGE="JavaScript">
<!—Hide from old browsers
//writes the date the document was saved
document.write(document.lastModified);
//end of the comment—>
</SCRIPT>
```

The hierarchy for this script starts with the top-level object *document* and its method *write*. The method's parentheses contain the object *document* and its property *lastModified*. The actual program gets the date the document was saved and writes it to the document after the text *This page was last modified*.

A third simple script that you can write opens a second Web document in a new window when the user clicks a button, as shown in Figures 6.3 and 6.4.

TEST OF SCRIPT

This page was last modified: 02/23/00 14:23:12

Figure 6.2 The date appears on the Web page

Figure 6.3 The button the user clicks to display the new window

Figure 6.4 The new window displays with the document

This script is an example of an event handler; that is, the JavaScript appears inside an HTML tag. To place the button on the Web page, use the <FORM> tags as follows:

```
<FORM>

<INPUT type="button" value="Oregon Ducks"
onClick="window.open('http://www.goducks.com')">

</FORM>
```

This script uses the HTML FORM INPUT type equals "button" to create a button that contains the text *Oregon Ducks*. The JavaScript onClick event handler opens the new window when the user clicks the button. The document designated by the URL is placed in the new window.

A fourth script could be used to place text in the status bar when the user points the mouse to linked text. For example, if you want to tell the user to bookmark your page before leaving to go to the GoDucks.com site, you would include the following script that makes use of the OnMouseOver and OnMouseOut events:

```
<A HREF="http://www.goducks.com"
onMouseOver="window.status='Please bookmark this site
before you leave!';return true"
onMouseOut="window.status='';return true">Oregon
Ducks</A>
```

Notice that the onMouseOut contains an empty opening and closing single quotation mark to remove the text from the status bar when the user moves the mouse off the link. Also notice the text *return true* that is used with the two event handlers. It is necessary to display the text in the status bar more than once. The result of this code is shown in Figure 6.5.

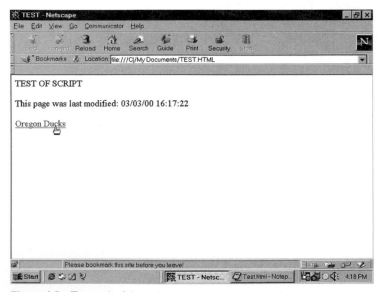

Figure 6.5 The result of the code

CREATING FUNCTIONS

The scripts we have created so far are simple lists of instructions that would occur once on the Web page. To extend your programming abilities, you can create JavaScript functions that group statements together for a particular purpose, and they can be used more than once on the page. Creating a function is a two-step process:

1. Define a function in the <HEAD> section.
2. Call the function from within the <BODY> of the document.

To define a function, you would use the following syntax:

```
<HEAD>
<SCRIPT LANGUAGE="JavaScript">
<!—hide from old browsers
//comment that describes the function
function name (parameter1, parameter2)
{
JavaScript statements
}
//end of comment—>
</SCRIPT>
</HEAD>
```

The previous example hides the JavaScript from old browsers and then places the word *function* in the script to declare that you are creating a function. The name of the function follows. You should name functions something meaningful, start the name with a character, and don't include any spaces in the name. If necessary, parameters, such as variables, can appear in the parentheses. The left-pointing brace ({) marks the beginning of the

JavaScript statements that the function will perform. The right-pointing brace (}) marks the end of the JavaScript statements and the end of the function.

To call the function once it is defined, you use the function's name in a <SCRIPT> tag or as an event handler as part of an HTML tag.

Suppose that you want your Web document to be responsive to users by allowing them to change the background color when they click on various buttons. Your script would need to place buttons on the screen changing the color scheme when the user clicks a button. Because each button would contain much of the same scripting, this example is a perfect candidate for a function because you can write the code once and call it several times. You would create the JavaScript as follows:

```
<HTML>
<HEAD>
<TITLE> JavaScript Test</TITLE>
<SCRIPT LANGUAGE="JavaScript">
<!—hide from old browsers
//the colorscheme function changes the background color
function colorscheme(bg)
{
document.bgColor=bg;
}
//End of Comment—>
</SCRIPT>
</HEAD>
<BODY>
<H1 ALIGN=CENTER>Test of Color Scheme
```

Function<H1>

Click a button to change the background color of the page.

<FORM>

<INPUT type="button" value="Yellow"
onClick="colorscheme(#FFFF00)">

<INPUT type="button" value="Green"
onClick="colorscheme(#00FF00)">

<INPUT type="button" value="Magenta"
onClick="colorscheme(#FF00FF)">

</FORM>

</BODY>

</HTML>

The results can be seen in Figures 6.6 and 6.7.

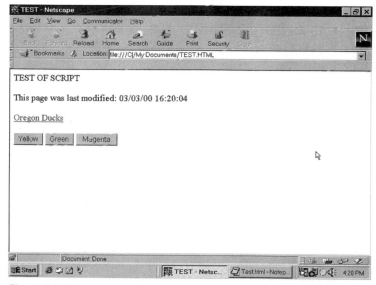

Figure 6.6   The page with the buttons

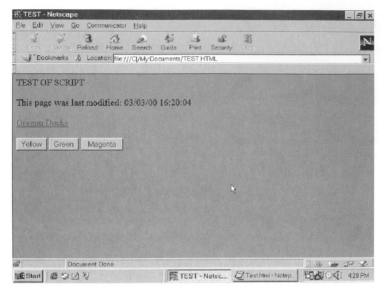

Figure 6.7   The page after the magenta button is clicked

Notice that the function makes use of a variable, which can be used to hold numbers or text. In this case the *bg* variable will be the color designated by the hexadecimal number that is passed to the function when the button is clicked.

TRY THIS! ADD A JAVASCRIPT SCRIPT TO YOUR WEB PAGE

☑   Using the design you created in the previous chapters, include a JavaScript alert box with text.

☑   Include a JavaScript script that places text on the screen.

☑   Include a JavaScript script that opens a new window that contains a document.

☑   Include a JavaScript script that places text in the status bar.

☑   Include a JavaScript script that calls a function when the mouse is clicked on an object.

ALPHABETIZED LIST OF HTML TAGS AND ATTRIBUTES USED IN THIS TEXT

Opening Tag	Closing Tag	Attributes	Description
<A>	</A>	NAME= HREF= SRC=	Defines a link and anchor in the same document or to an external file
<ADDRESS>	</ADDRESS>		Places the name or email address of the owner or designer of the Web page
<B>	</B>		Boldfaces text
<BASEFONT>		SIZE=	Changes the size of the font for the entire document
<BLINK>	</BLINK>		Makes text blink
<BODY>	</BODY>	BGCOLOR= BACKGROUND= TEXT= LINK= VLINK= ALINK=	Defines the body of the Web document
 			Line break
<CENTER>	</CENTER>		Centers text
<EM>	</EM>		Emphasizes text
<FONT>	</FONT>	SIZE=	Changes an font size
<FORM>	</FORM>	ACTION= METHOD=	Creates an interactive form
<FRAME>	</FRAME>	NAME NORESIZE SRC SCROLLING	Sets up contents of frames
<FRAMESET>	</FRAMESET>	ROWS= COLS=	Sets up frames in an HTML document
<H1>...<H6>	</H1>...</H6>		Formats text in headings
<HEAD>	</HEAD>		First section of HTML document
<HR>		SIZE= WIDTH=	Creates a horizontal rule or line
<HTML>	</HTML>		Encloses the entire Web document
<I>	</I>		Italicizes text
<IMG>		SRC= ALT= WIDTH= HEIGHT=	Places an image in the document

Opening Tag	Closing Tag	Attributes	Description
<INPUT>		TYPE= SIZE= NAME= MAXLENGTH= VALUE=	Specifies input type for interactive form
<LI>			Starts each line of an ordered or unordered list
<META>		NAME= CONTENT=	Placed in head section to identify page to search engines
<NOFRAMES>	</NOFRAMES>		Places text in document for those who can't view frames
<OL>	</OL>		Creates an ordered or numbered list
<OPTION>			Identifies each menu item on a form within the <SELECT> tags
<P>	</P>		Starts a new paragraph
<SCRIPT>	</SCRIPT>	LANGUAGE SRC	Container used to hold a JavaScript program
<SELECT>	</SELECT>		Defines a dropdown menu on a form
<STRIKE>	</STRIKE>		Strikes out text
<STRONG>	</STRONG>		Strongly emphasizes text
<STYLE>	</STYLE>	TAG TO BE REDEFINED	Sets up styles for the current document
_			Subscripts text
[	]		Superscripts text
<TABLE>	</TABLE>	BORDER CELLSPACING= CELLPADDING=	Encloses entire table
<TD>	</TD>		Encloses a cell in a table that contains data
<TEXTAREA>	</TEXTAREA>	COLS= ROWS=	Defines a text area on a form
<TH>	</TH>		Encloses a cell in a table that contains a heading
<TITLE>	</TITLE>		Must appear in head section—identifies entire page
<TR>	</TR>		Encloses each row of a table
<U>	</U>		Underlines text
<UL>	</UL>		Creates an unordered or bulleted list